LABORATORY TECH

COLORING BOOK

THIS BOOK BELONGS TO:

____

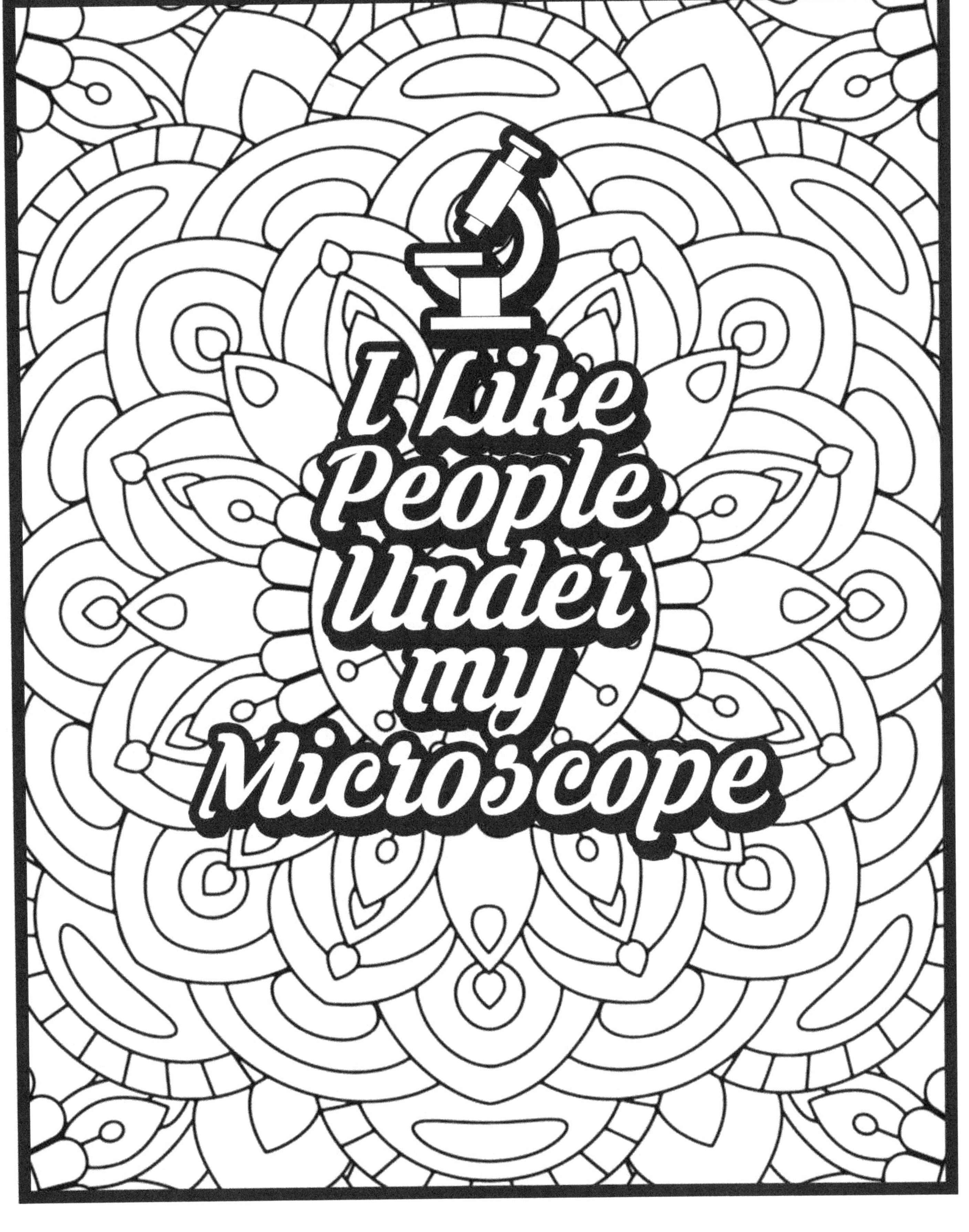
I Like
People
Under
my
Microscope

STOP
STARING
AT MY RACK

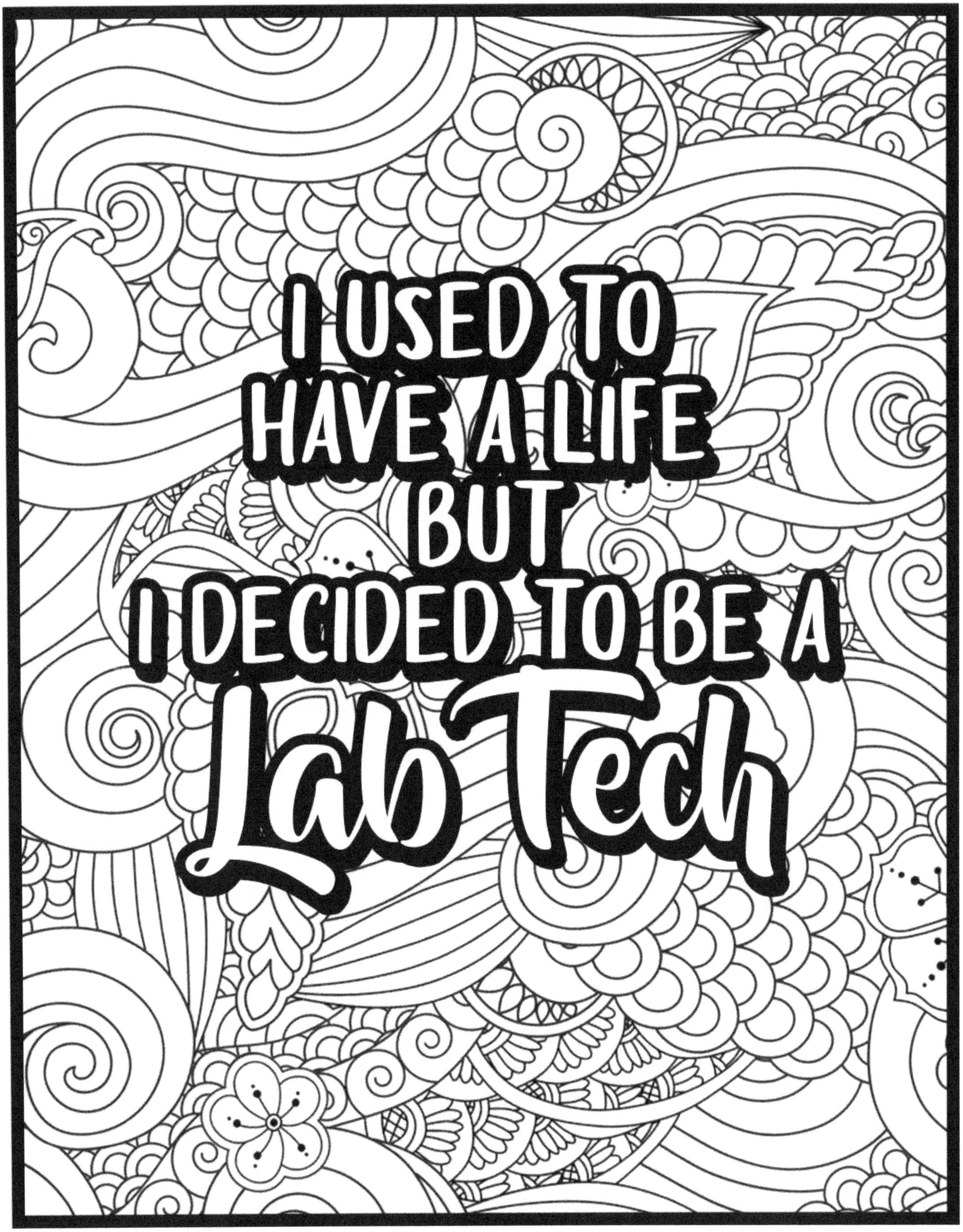
I USED TO
HAVE A LIFE
BUT
I DECIDED TO BE A
Lab Tech

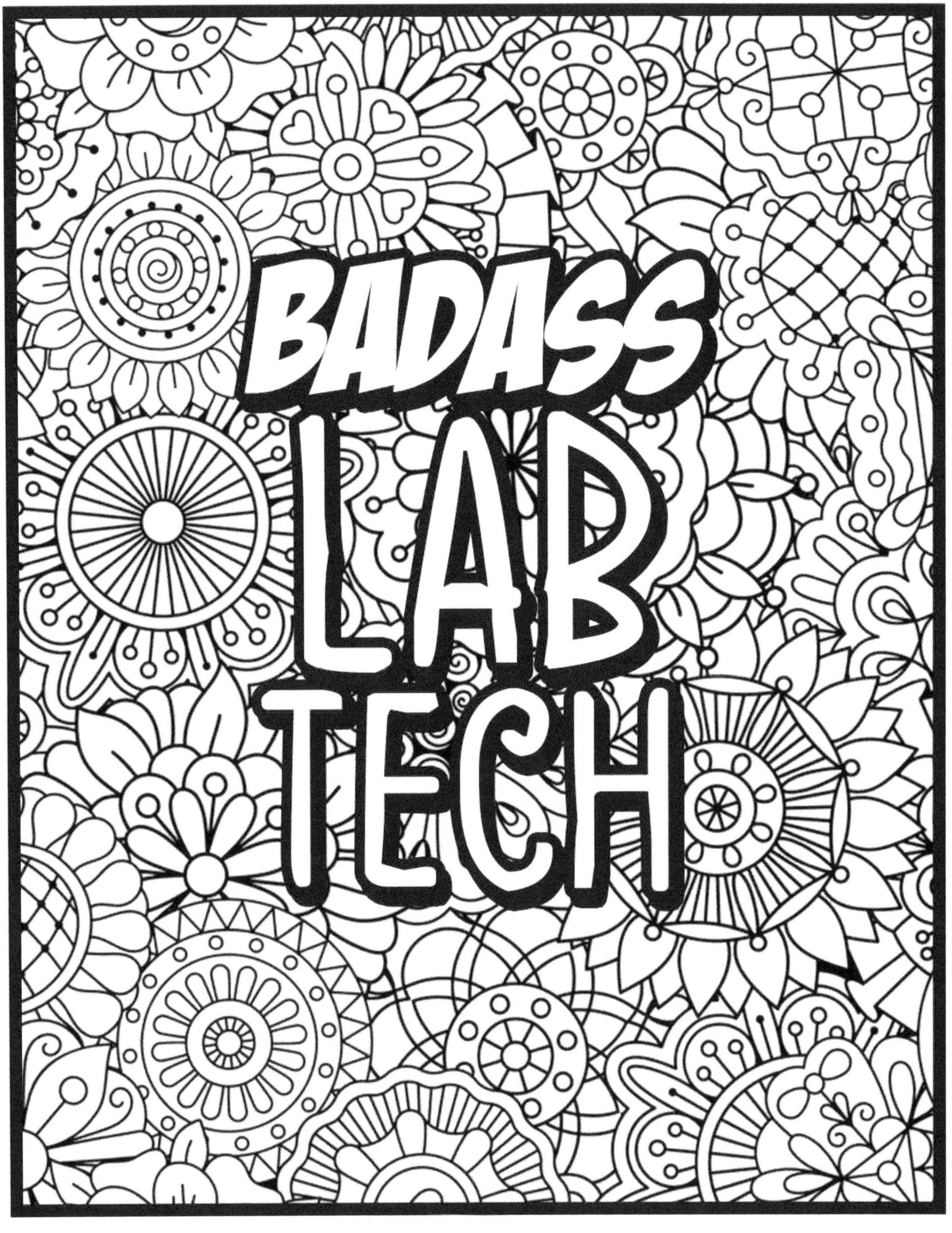
BADASS
LAB
TECH

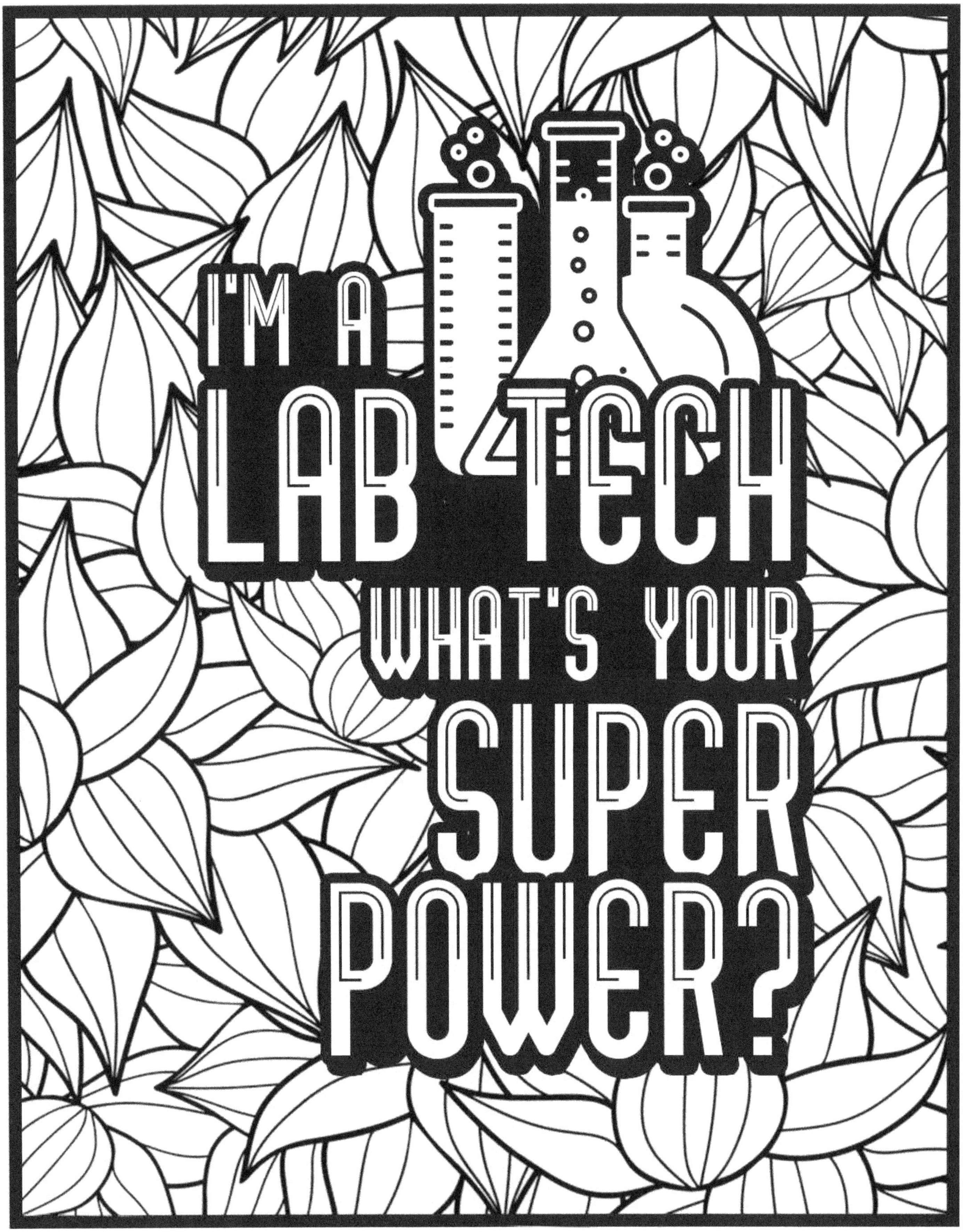
I'M A
LAB TECH
WHAT'S YOUR
SUPER
POWER?

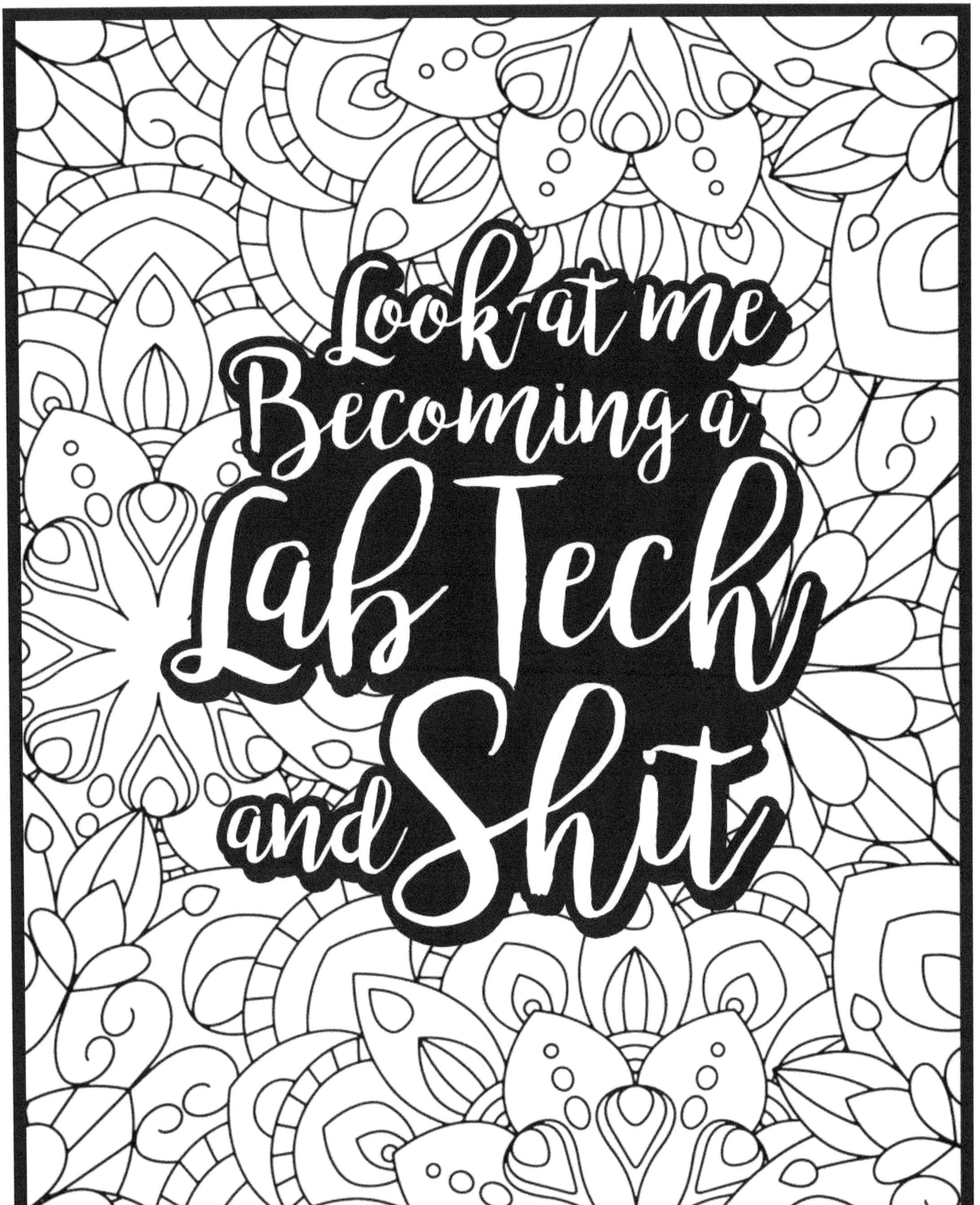
Look at me
Becoming a
Lab Tech
and Shit

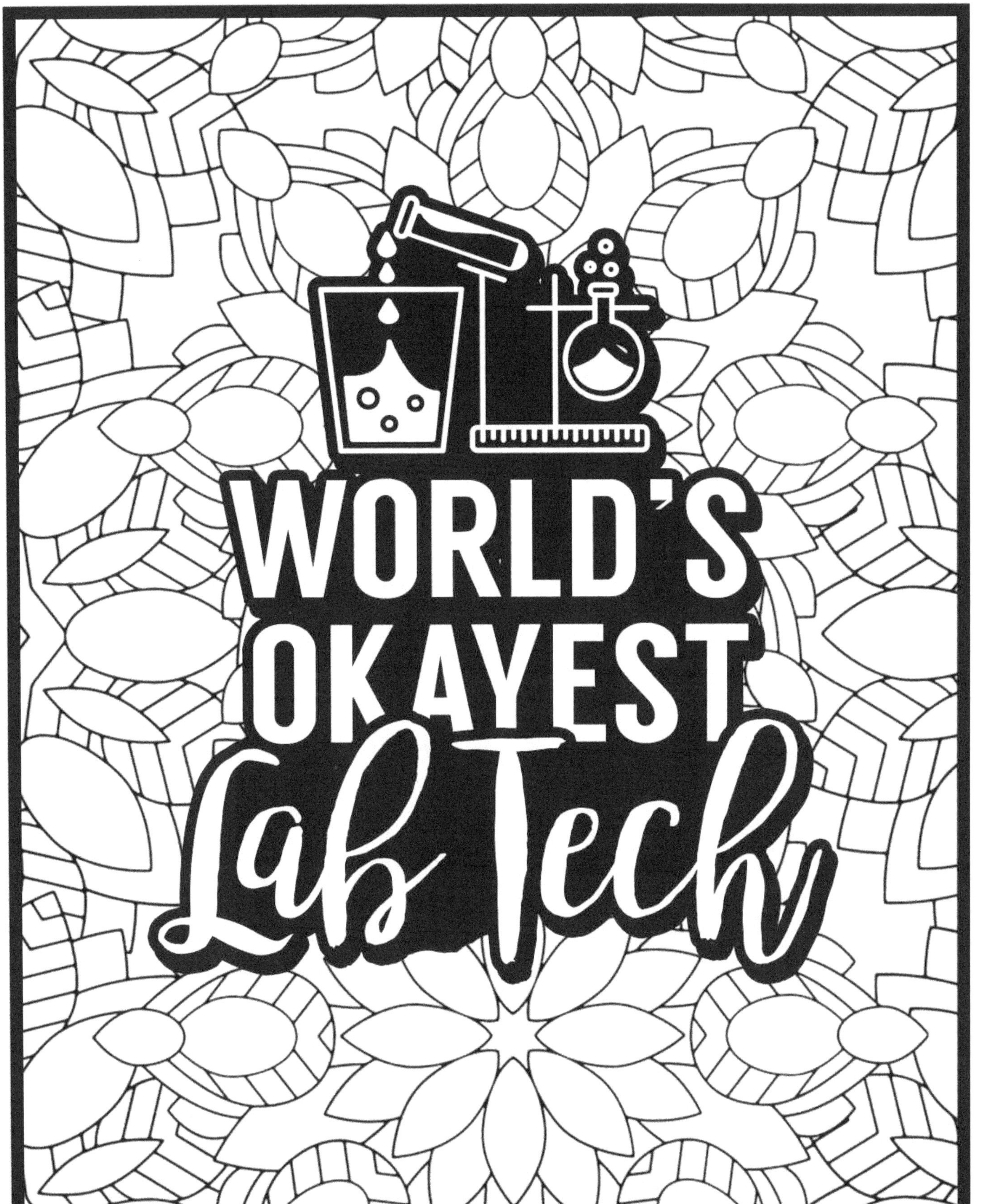
WORLD'S
OKAYEST
Lab Tech

I CAN
CHANGE
THE
WORLD

BORN
TO
Pipette

WHAT
THE
ACTUAL
FUCK?

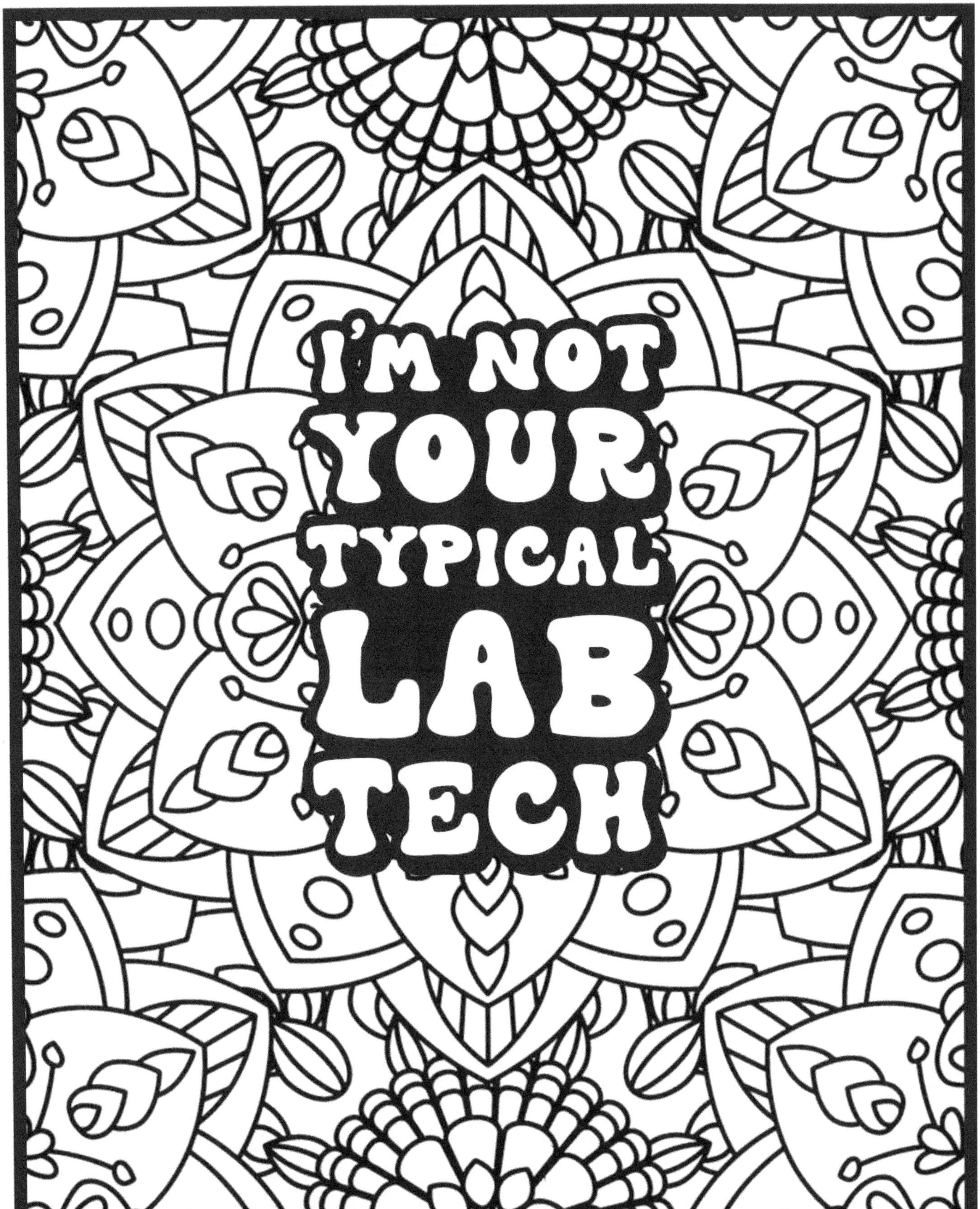
I'M NOT
YOUR
TYPICAL
LAB
TECH

L V E

Shit
Happens

CHEMISTRY
IS LIKE COOKING
JUST DON'T
LICK
THE SPOON

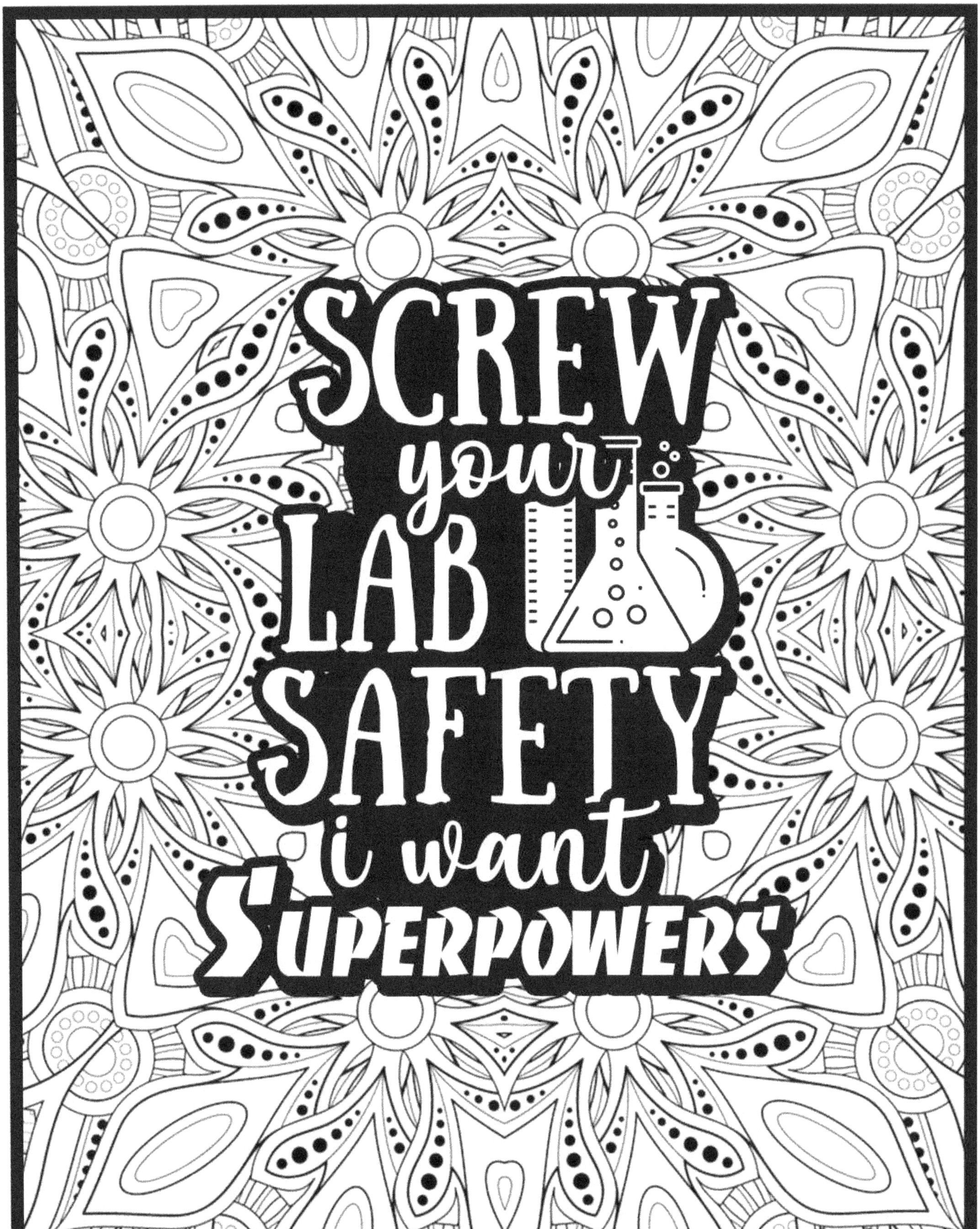
SCREW
your
LAB
SAFETY
i want
SUPERPOWERS

I'll Touch
Anything
AS LONG AS I HAVE
Gloves On

BACTERIA
THE ONLY
CULTURE
SOME PEOPLE
WILL EVER
HAVE

IF YOU SEE ME
RUNNING
Try
TO KEEP UP

ALCOHOL
IS A SOLUTION
ACCORDING TO
CHEMISTRY

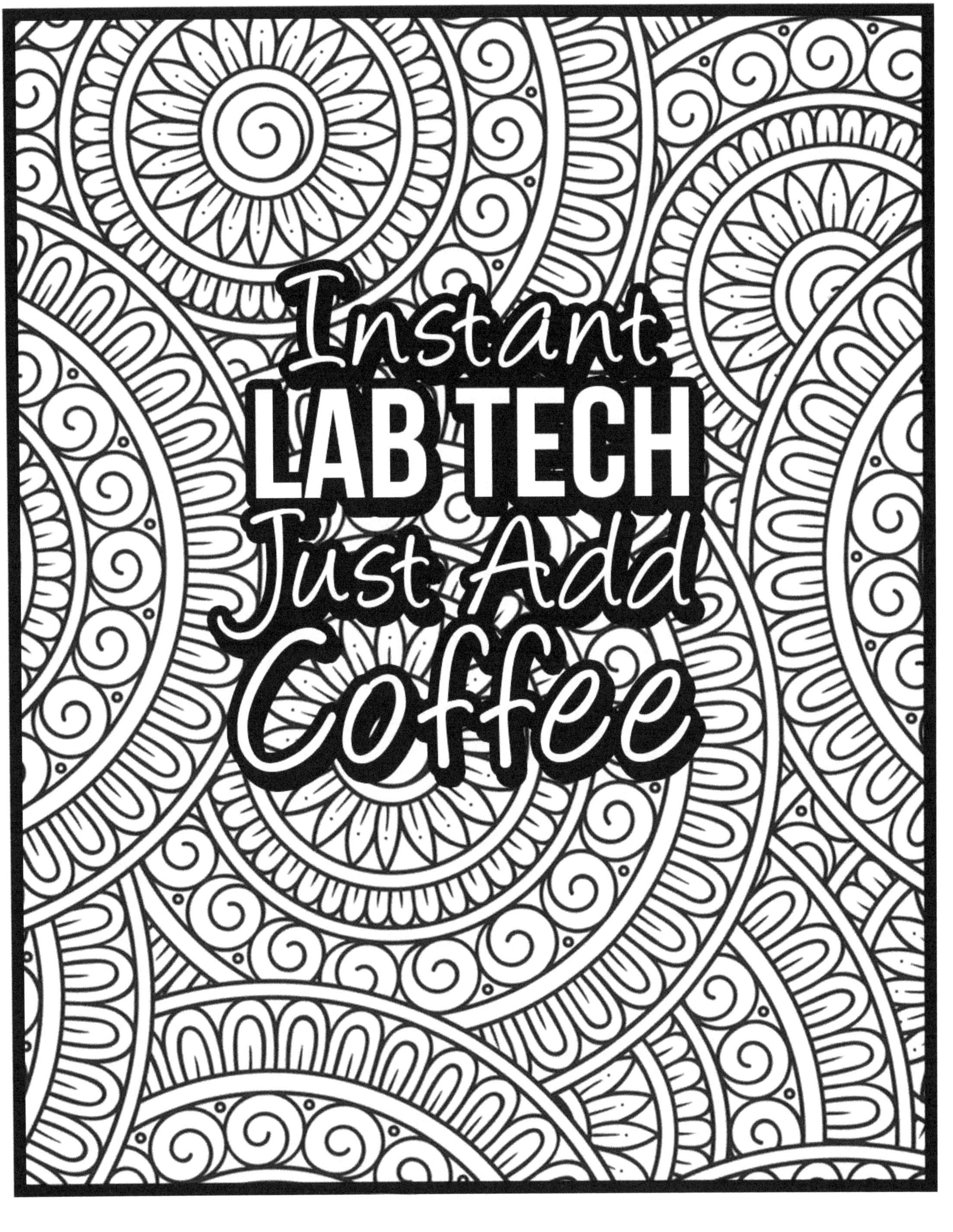
Instant
LAB TECH
Just Add
Coffee

CPSIA information can be obtained
at www.ICGtesting.com
Printed in the USA
LVHW060209010323
740673LV00012B/693

9 798729 675760